DEBUNKING HISTORY

THE REAL STORY BEHIND THE

AGE OF EXPLORATION

DANIEL R. FAUST

PowerKiDS press

New York

Published in 2020 by The Rosen Publishing Group, Inc.
29 East 21st Street, New York, NY 10010

First Edition

Editor: Jill Keppeler
Book Design: Reann Nye

Photo Credits: Cover SuperStock/Getty Images; pp. 5, 9, 11 (bottom) Everett Historical/Shutterstock.com; p. 6 https://commons.wikimedia.org/wiki/File:Portrait_of_a_Man,_Said_to_be_Christopher_Columbus.jpg; pp. 7, 29 (top) DEA PICTURE LIBRARY/ De Agostini/Getty Images; p. 8 https://commons.wikimedia.org/wiki/File:Irving-Washington-LOC.jpg; p. 11 (Isabel I) https://commons.wikimedia.org/wiki/File:Isabel_I_of_Castile.jpg; p. 11 (Ferdinand II) https://commons.wikimedia.org/wiki/File:Michel_Sittow_004.jpg; p. 12 Ivan Marc/Shutterstock.com; p. 13 (top) Heritage Images/ Hulton Fine Art Collection/Getty Images; p. 13 (bottom) Ricardo Bacchini/Shutterstock.com; p. 15 Bernhard Richter/Shutterstock.com; p. 16 Esteban De Armas/Shutterstock.com; p. 17 (top) Science & Society Picture Library/SSPL/Getty Images; p. 17 (bottom) VW Pics/ Universal Images Group/Getty Images; p. 19 Historical Picture Archive/ Corbis Historical/Getty Images; p. 21 (top) WitR/Shutterstock.com; p. 21 (bottom) https://en.wikipedia.org/wiki/File:Hern%C3%A1n_Cort%C3%A9s_(Museo_del_Prado).jpg; p. 22 Stock Montage/ Archive Photos/Getty Images; pp. 23, 25 Bettmann/Getty Images; p. 27 (bottom) Pavel Svoboda Photography/Shutterstock.com; p. 27 (top) https://commons.wikimedia.org/wiki/File:1635_Blaeu_Map_Guiana,_Venezuela,_and_El_Dorado_-_Geographicus_-_Guiana-blaeu-1635.jpg; p. 29 (bottom) https://commons.wikimedia.org/wiki/File:Fur_traders_in_canada_1777.jpg.

Cataloging-in-Publication Data

Names: Faust, Daniel R.
Title: The real story behind the age of exploration / Daniel R. Faust.
Description: New York : PowerKids Press, 2020. | Series: The real story: debunking history | Includes glossary and index.
Identifiers: ISBN 9781538344606 (pbk.) | ISBN 9781538343425 (library bound) | ISBN 9781538344613 (6 pack)
Subjects: LCSH: Discoveries in geography–Juvenile literature. | Explorers–Juvenile literature.
Classification: LCC G175.F38 2020 | DDC 910.9–dc23

Manufactured in the United States of America

CPSIA Compliance Information: Batch #CSPK19. For Further Information contact Rosen Publishing, New York, New York at 1-800-237-9932

CONTENTS

SETTING SAIL

People are curious by nature. Throughout history, people have wanted to know what was around the next corner or over the next mountain. Our natural curiosity has led humanity to explore many parts of our planet and beyond.

A period of time starting in the 15th century and lasting more than 100 years is sometimes called the Age of Exploration or the Age of Discovery. During this time, explorers from several European countries took advantage of the scientific discoveries of the Renaissance and set sail to see what was over the horizon.

We're taught that the goal of the Age of Exploration was to discover new lands and find new trade routes. Much of what we know about the Age of Exploration is told from the **perspective** of the Europeans. That's only part of the story.

Our natural curiosity has led us to explore much of our planet, from the highest mountains to the deepest seas. It's even led us to outer space, the moon, and perhaps, one day, Mars.

FLAT OR ROUND?

You may have heard stories about people from the 15th and 16th centuries believing Earth was flat. Some people say that Christopher Columbus set sail to prove Earth was round or that he had to convince the crews of his ships that they wouldn't sail off the edge of the world if they traveled too far west. This makes for an exciting story, but is it true?

Many ancient civilizations, from Greece to China, believed Earth was flat. Some showed Earth as a disk, or a flat, circular shape, surrounded by a large body of water. By the time Columbus set sail in 1492, however, people had known Earth was round for hundreds of years. So how did these stories get started?

CHRISTOPHER COLUMBUS

Ancient maps, such as those created by the Greek historian and geographer Hecataeus, often showed the world as a disk where the known lands floated on a large, circular ocean. This map is based on his work.

The ancient Greeks figured out Earth is round thousands of years ago. About 350 BC, Aristotle wrote *On the Heavens*, in which he recorded his astronomical theories, including that Earth is a large **sphere**. Not long after, Eratosthenes, a Greek scientist and astronomer, estimated the **circumference** of Earth by comparing the angle of the sun's rays at the same time in two different cities. The people of Columbus's time accepted a spherical Earth as fact.

A story that Columbus planned to prove Earth was round may have first appeared in the early 1800s. In 1828, American writer Washington Irving wrote *The Life and Voyages of Christopher Columbus*, a mostly fictional tale of Columbus's life. Irving falsely claimed Columbus's voyages helped prove Earth wasn't flat.

WASHINGTON IRVING

Many of the scientific books that European explorers would have read clearly stated that Earth was a sphere.

VIKINGS AND MONKS

In 1937, President Franklin D. Roosevelt made October 12 a federal holiday called Columbus Day. Since 1971, Columbus Day has been celebrated on the second Monday of October. Some people consider the voyage of Christopher Columbus an important part of the American story. Students learn about him in school. But what do they learn?

Hoping to find a sea route to Asia, Columbus convinced the king and queen of Spain to finance voyages across the Atlantic Ocean. In 1492, Columbus arrived in the Americas, probably in the Bahamas. After that, he mistook Cuba for Japan. Over the course of three more voyages, Columbus landed at various locations in the Americas, including the coast of Venezuela. He never, however, landed in North America.

FERDINAND AND ISABELLA

King Ferdinand II of Aragon and Queen Isabella I of Castile, also known as the Catholic Monarchs, were the rulers who paid for Columbus's voyages. Their marriage was the first step toward unifying the kingdom of Spain. They were interested in expanding the power of the new Spanish Empire, as well as spreading Christianity around the world.

QUEEN ISABELLA I

KING FERDINAND II

Even if Christopher Columbus was the first European to make it to the Americas, he didn't truly discover something new. Millions of people already lived there in thriving civilizations.

Many people believe that Christopher Columbus was the first European to make it to the so-called New World, but is that true? Probably not. There is a good deal of evidence (including the remains of a settlement in what is now Newfoundland, Canada) that the Vikings beat Columbus to the New World by about 500 years.

About AD 1000, a Viking explorer called Leif Eriksson sailed west from Norway, headed to the Viking settlement in Greenland. Instead, Eriksson eventually landed in Canada. The Vikings made several voyages to North America for timber and other natural resources. After about 10 years, however, the Vikings apparently stopped visiting.

LEIF ERIKSSON

FACT FINDER

Some stories say that, about AD 500, an Irish monk now called Saint Brendan sailed west in a boat made of leather, eventually reaching North America. However, there is no evidence of this.

Leif Eriksson came from a family of famous Viking explorers. His father, Erik the Red, founded the first Viking settlement on Greenland.

GREENLAND

HERE THERE BE DRAGONS

So, you might think, even though Columbus didn't prove Earth was round and wasn't the first European to discover the Americas, at least he did find what Europeans considered a New World. He must have known this was something special. Nope. In fact, historians say Columbus died believing that he'd found a new route to Asia.

However, explorers who came after him knew the truth. The Americas were entirely new to them, and many people were fascinated. They were, however, also cautious. Mapmakers of the time sometimes used **fantastic** animals and monsters as decorations around the borders of their maps. These animals were also used as warnings. Encounters with strange and dangerous new animals were a very real threat when exploring unknown territory.

FACT FINDER

People of the Age of Exploration knew very little about what lived in the deep seas or these new (to them) lands. The Atlantic Ocean was known as "the Sea of Darkness."

Elephant skulls have a single, large hole in the center. Some experts believe people may have mistaken this hole for a single eye socket, or opening, creating the myth of the Cyclops, a one-eyed monster. Other elephant bones have been mistaken for the bones of giants.

However fantastic they seem now, some of the animals on old maps were believed to be quite real. Stories of strange animals in the ocean have led to any number of legends. The tusk of the narwhal, a member of the whale family, may have been used as proof that unicorns exist.

Viking sailors in the North Atlantic used to tell stories about a monster called a kraken. This giant sea creature could crush ships with its powerful arms, create powerful currents and whirlpools, and even swallow an entire ship's crew in a single gulp! Today, many scientists believe that the stories of the kraken were inspired by a real animal, the giant squid. These animals can grow to a length of 43 feet (13.1 m), including two long tentacles.

KRAKEN

NARWHAL TUSK

Vikings traded narwhal tusks with travelers from southern Europe and the Mediterranean, knowing that those travelers thought the long tooth was really the horn of a unicorn.

DIFFERENT CIVILIZATIONS

Given that he has a U.S. holiday named for him, it would be easy to assume Columbus and other explorers were heroes. This isn't really true. While Columbus did open up the so-called New World for European exploration, many people were already living there before he "found" it. These societies, however, were not necessarily the type European explorers recognized as civilized by their standards.

Most of what we know about the first encounters between European explorers and the **indigenous** peoples of other areas comes from the reports made by the explorers themselves. They often wrote about people who wore little clothing, lived in simple houses, and used stone tools and weapons. To European eyes, this made the native inhabitants inferior and uncivilized.

FACT FINDER

A vast trade network existed among the different native groups of North America long before the first Europeans arrived. These tribes were happy to trade with the Europeans—at least, at first.

Columbus nearly immediately took some of the native peoples of the Americas as slaves. Over his time there, he enslaved thousands.

Long before the Europeans began to arrive in numbers, Native Americans had developed **complex** civilizations with cities, temples, and monuments that rivaled or **surpassed** many European civilizations of the time. An advanced society called the Mississippian **culture** developed across what is now the central and southeastern United States about 800 years before Columbus arrived. The Mississippian culture built large burial mounds and grew maize (a type of corn) and other crops.

There were many complex societies in Central America, including those of the Olmecs, Maya, Toltecs, and Aztecs. By the time the first Europeans arrived, two native empires—the Aztecs in Central America and the Inca in South America—still existed in the area. The Spanish were amazed by Tenochtitlán, the capital of the Aztec Empire, when they arrived in 1519.

HERNÁN CORTÉS

Hernán Cortés is renowned as an explorer, but he's also known for the **brutality** with which he destroyed the Aztec civilization. Cortés was born in 1485 in western Spain. In 1504, he sailed to the Americas, where he assisted in the violent Spanish **conquest** of Cuba. In 1519, Cortés led an expedition into Mexico, which he had heard contained great wealth. Cortés and his soldiers eventually defeated the Aztecs and destroyed Tenochtitlán.

Tenochtitlán had about 400,000 residents in 1519. The city had many canals and a huge marketplace where the people gathered to buy and sell items. Mexico City was built on its ruins.

HERNÁN CORTÉS

MAN OR GOD?

Some stories tell that when Hernán Cortés arrived in the territory of the Aztecs, their leader, Montezuma II, thought he was the god Quetzalcoatl or another god. Aztec prophecies, these tales tell, said a white-skinned god would arrive from the East. These stories say that the Aztec leader welcomed Cortés because of this mistake.

In truth, there's no reason to believe Montezuma thought Cortés was a god in any way. Cortés didn't mention being mistaken for Quetzalcoatl in any of his letters. He does say Montezuma gave a welcoming speech to the invaders, claiming that the Aztecs had been waiting for the return of a past ruler, but Cortés almost certainly made this speech up. The stories about Quetzalcoatl arose later.

MONTEZUMA II

People sometimes make up stories such as the one about Cortés and Quetzalcoatl to make it look like the natives were silly and superstitious or to justify how the explorers took over their land.

THE FOUNTAIN OF YOUTH

Many people know the story of Juan Ponce de León and his search for the fountain of youth. Throughout history, there have been many legends about waters that give eternal life. However, nothing really connected Ponce de León with any of these legends until years after he died.

Like many explorers of the time, Ponce de León was most interested in finding new land and the wealth that came with it. He helped establish a Spanish colony on Hispaniola, which is modern-day Haiti and the Dominican Republic. He sailed to Puerto Rico in search of gold and was named governor when it became a Spanish colony. Ponce de León was also the first European to find Florida, which he named.

THE TAINO PEOPLE

The Tainos were an indigenous people in the Caribbean at the time of Columbus's arrival in 1492. They lived in what are now Cuba, Jamaica, Puerto Rico, Haiti, and the Dominican Republic. They grew yams and a plant called cassava and hunted birds, lizards, and other small animals. When the Spanish arrived, there were about 2 million Taino people living in the Caribbean. By 1550, they were nearly **extinct**.

FACT FINDER

None of Ponce de León's letters mention a fountain of youth. Some scholars think a rival invented the story later to make the explorer look foolish.

This picture shows Juan Ponce de León receiving water from the fountain of youth. It's still a popular story.

EL DORADO

One of the main reasons Europeans ventured across the ocean during the Age of Exploration was to find wealth, especially gold. When Spanish explorers first arrived in South America in the 1500s, they heard stories of a civilization high in the Andes. This society was said to have a chief who covered himself in gold dust when he became ruler. El Dorado, which means "**gilded** one," was the name given to this legendary chief.

However, at some point over the years, the name shifted to mean the city of great golden wealth that the Europeans believed was hidden somewhere in South America. They searched for this legendary city (and a number of others) but never discovered it. Today, the name is used for any place said to contain great wealth.

FACT FINDER

Stories also said the legendary people of El Dorado threw gold and precious jewels into a lake to worship an underwater god.

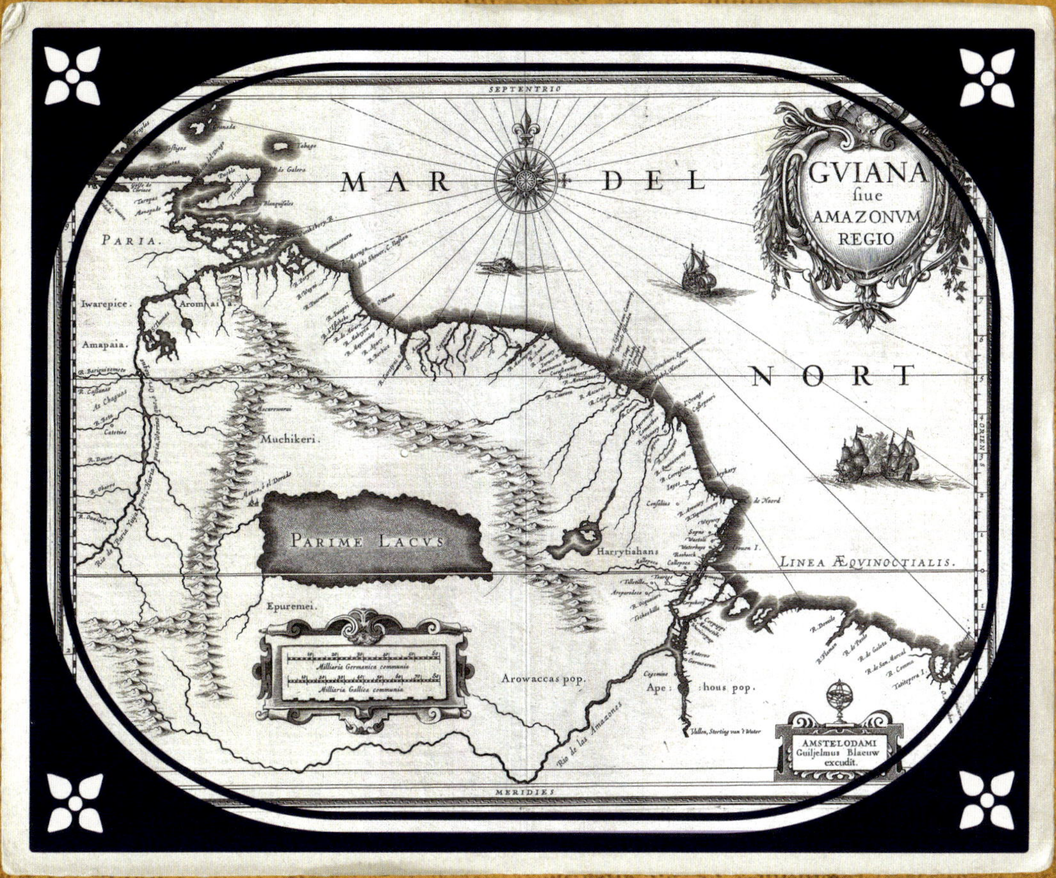

Although there is no such thing as El Dorado, many maps drawn by European explorers, like this one from 1635, claim to show the city's location or a route to it.

THE ANDES

DISEASES AND DESTRUCTION

While fighting between European explorers and the people who already lived in the Americas killed many Native Americans, disease probably did far more damage. When the Europeans invaded, they brought diseases such as measles, smallpox, and the flu. The native peoples had little or no immunity against these illnesses. Some experts estimate up to 95 percent of the native population of the Americas died in the years immediately following the Europeans' arrival.

In addition, we don't always consider the wider **environmental** damage the Europeans caused. Europeans assumed the New World would provide an endless supply of natural resources. They cut down forests to make room for farmland and to provide timber for buildings. Beavers and other animals were nearly hunted to extinction.

TO BEAVER OR NOT TO BEAVER

Beaver fur was highly prized in Europe. It was so popular that people almost hunted the European beaver to extinction. When Dutch, French, and British explorers arrived in North America and saw the large populations of beavers, they quickly began trapping them and trading with the Native Americans for their furs. Before Europeans arrived, there were 60 million to 400 million beavers in North American. By the 1900s, there were only about 100,000.

Tenochtitlán had so many people that smallpox spread very quickly. That's a big reason why Cortés was able to take the city.

FUR TRADERS IN CANADA

FACT VS. FICTION

Everyone loves a good story, and history is full of great stories. But history is more than just a tale. History is a record of events that actually happened and the people who took part in those events. As exciting as the stories of the Age of Exploration might be, we must be careful not to ignore the facts behind the events.

A lot of the history you've learned in school was probably written from the perspective of European men. However, many different types of people have shaped history. Strong civilizations thrived in the Americas long before the Europeans "discovered" these continents. Instead of taking the history you've learned at face value, it's always good to see if there's more to the story.

GLOSSARY

brutality: Violent, harsh treatment.

circumference: The length of a line that goes around the middle of a spere.

complex: Not easy to understand or explain; having many parts.

conquest: Taking control of an area by force.

culture: The beliefs and ways of life of a certain group of people.

environmental: Having to do with the natural world.

extinct: No longer existing.

fantastic: Very strange or unusual.

gild: To cover in gold.

indigenous: Living naturally in a particular region.

perspective: Point of view.

sphere: A ball or something shaped like a ball.

surpass: To be greater than or better than something.

INDEX

WEBSITES

Due to the changing nature of Internet links, PowerKids Press has developed an online list of websites related to the subject of this book. This site is updated regularly. Please use this link to access the list: www.powerkidslinks.com/debunk/explorers